BIRDS

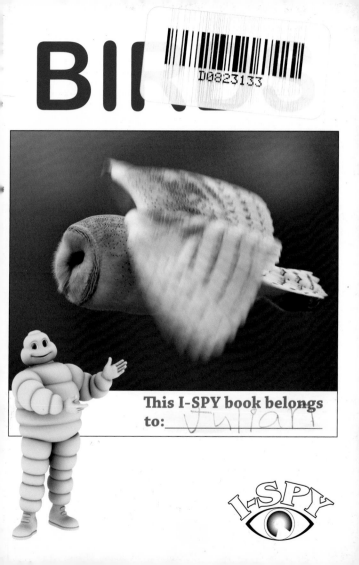

This I-SPY book belongs
to: Julian

I-SPY

Introduction

Bird watching is one of our most popular pastimes and it is easy to see why. By some estimates there are more than 11,000 different kinds of birds that have been identified throughout the world. Britain alone can boast a list of more than 400 species. The RSPB (The Royal Society for the Protection of Birds) does a great job in identifying species at risk in the UK and protecting them to increase their numbers. They operate a priority listing, with their 'red list' showing those birds most at risk.

Although the basic body shape of all birds remains the same, there is a wide variety of sizes. Wings and tails come in different shapes and sizes, as do legs and beaks. And these variations reflect the kind of habitat in which the bird lives as well as the type of food it eats and other aspects of its behaviour. Birds' songs are often a joy to listen to as they claim their territories in the spring.

Every song is different and with patience, it is possible to identify many birds without seeing them at all. You do not even need to stray from your house and garden to enjoy watching the antics of Tits at a bag of nuts, House Sparrows dust bathing or Blackbirds tugging away at a resistant worm in the lawn. Finally, by setting out the right kinds of food and water, it is possible to attract many different sorts of birds to your garden so that in a way, your garden becomes an 'unofficial' bird reserve.

How to use your I-SPY book

The birds in this book are arranged in much the same way as in most identification guides. In most cases, the male birds are illustrated as females are often more drably coloured.

You need 1000 points to send off for your I-Spy certificate (see page 64) but that is not too difficult because there are masses of points in every book. As you make each l-Spy, write your score in the box and where there is a question, double your score if you can answer it. Check your answer against the correct one on page 63.

CANADA GOOSE

As their name suggests, these well-known geese originally came from North America but they were introduced into Europe more than 200 years ago. You can see them on lakes and ponds or in fields.

I-SPY points: 10

Date: _____

MALLARD

Everyone knows the Mallard. It is the bird that you always think of as a typical wild duck.

Ducks and drakes look identical. True or False?

I-SPY points: 5
Double with answer

Date: _____

MANDARIN DUCK

Originally from China, this beautiful bird has thankfully, escaped from private collections of ornamental wildfowl and now adorns our lakes and slower rivers. It's unusual for a duck as it nests in holes in trees.

I-SPY points: 20

Date: _____

POCHARD

The Pochard is a striking bird that regularly visits the Ponds and Lakes in London's Royal Parks however, its preferred home is flooded gravel pits and other large lakes.

I-SPY points: 25

Date: _____

DUNNOCK

Often seen around hedges and wrongly called the Hedge Sparrow it is not related to sparrows, the two birds have different beak shapes and different food requirements. They are often seen quietly and efficiently picking up scraps under the bird table.

I-SPY points: 10

Date: _____

4

WREN

This is a tiny bird and, although it is very common, its habit of hiding in hedges and holes in banks makes it hard to see. Its Latin name of Troglodytes means 'cave dweller'. For such a small bird, it has a very loud song.

I-SPY points: 15

Date: _____

STARLING

One of the Starlings most noticeable characteristics is that in winter, in special places, roosting flocks of millions are a daily spectacle! Also, it's an excellent mimic - phones and alarms are a speciality!

I-SPY points: 10

Date: _____

HOUSE SPARROW

Everyone can recognize this little bird because it is found so close to houses and farms. It will readily feed on household scraps and seeds from the bird table as well as insects.

I-SPY points: 15

Date:_____

LONG-TAILED TIT

I-SPY points: 10

Date:_____

With its plump little body and long tail, this delightful member of the tit family is easy to recognize. It is found in woodland and hedgerows.

COAL TIT

The Coal Tit has a black cap with a white patch in it. These birds are usually found in mixed woodlands and in winter form mixed species flocks to visit bird tables and feeders.

I-SPY points: 15

Date: _____

BLUE TIT

A popular garden visitor, these little birds are familar because of their acrobatics at bird feeders. A gardeners friend, they eat more aphids (small plant eating insects) than any other species.

I-SPY points: 5

Date: _____

GREAT TIT

With its blue-black head, white cheek patches, and yellow breast with a black bar down the centre, this is an easy bird to identify. The male's 'teacherteacher' song is also a familiar spring sound.

I-SPY points: 5

Date: _____

SWIFT

With their long, sickle-shaped wings and fast, agile flight, these birds are well named. Listen for their shrill scream - made at breakneck speed just feet above the ground or high in the sky. Swifts have been known to stay aloft for two to three years years without landing.

I-SPY points: 15

Date:

HOUSE MARTIN

It is the white bar at the base of the tail which will allow you to distinguish these birds from Swallows or Swifts.

When they do not nest on houses, where would you expect them to build their nests?

I-SPY points: 15

Double with answer

Date:

PIED WAGTAIL

Pied Wagtails are black and white and its plumage make this bird hard to miss. It's always rushing about flicking its tail while searching for insects. It's not just a countryside bird; in fact, it often roosts in large numbers in cities.

I-SPY points: 5

Date: _____

ROBIN

Some books suggest that it is only the male Robin which has the familiar red breast. This is quite untrue and the sexes are almost impossible to tell apart.

Robins have an autumn/ winter song and a spring/ summer song. True or False?

I-SPY points: 5

Double with answer

Date: _____

BLACKBIRD

With his shiny black plumage, yellow beak, and yellow ring round his eye, the male Blackbird is a handsome bird. The female is a dull brown colour. The male's song is musical.

I-SPY points: 5

Date: _____

CHAFFINCH

This is a very familiar bird, and the male's colours of bluish, pink, brown, green, and white stand out. The female has roughly the same pattern but the colours are duller.

I-SPY points: 5

Date: _____

GREENFINCH

The male bird is a bright yellowish green while the female is rather duller. Look for these birds in woodland, along hedgerows, in parks, and even in your garden.

I-SPY points: 5

Date: _____

GOLDFINCH

The bright red, white, black, and yellow colours of this delightful little finch make it easy to recognize. It is often seen feeding on the seeds of thistle heads in autumn.

I-SPY points: 10

Date: _____

BRAMBLING

More than a million of these colourful finches arrive in the UK in late September. They are about the same size as a Chaffinch with whom they often form large flocks.

I-SPY points: 30

Date: _____

GREAT CRESTED GREBE

This attractive bird breeds on lakes, gravel pits, and sometimes on rivers. Look out for the head tufts during the breeding season.

I-SPY points: 15

Date: _____

MOORHEN

Moorhens are found in most kinds of watery areas where there are plants growing. Sometimes they may be quite shy. Look out for the red area on the front of the head and base of the beak and the constantly flicking white tail.

I-SPY points: 10

Date: _____

COOT

'As bald as a coot'! or so the saying goes, but Coots are not bald but they do have a white patch on the forehead and beak. They are found on lakes, gravel pits, and reservoirs.

I-SPY points: 10

Date: _____

PINTAIL

Larger than a mallard, its pointed wings and tapering tail make it easy to distinguish from other ducks. They live in marshy ground while breeding and move to estuaries during winter to join the many thousands that migrate from Europe.

I-SPY points: 30

Date: _____

GOLDENEYE

Spotting a Goldeneye is getting easier; they are now quite common in winter around inland waterways and marshes. Rather unusually for ducks, they nest in trees and are being encouraged to nest in special nestboxes so that we have them here all year round.

I-SPY points: 25

Date: _____

TUFTED DUCK

This black and white duck gets its name from the tuft on its head. They can be found in great numbers on lakes, reservoirs, and flooded gravel pits.

I-SPY points: 10

Date:

SHOVELER

An unmistakable duck, its wide, flat specialised bill enables it to filter feed on weed, crustaceans and small insects at the waters edge. It prefers areas of deep cover and outside of the breeding season even the drake (male) is actually quite drab. The best place to see a Shoveler would be a nature reserve during winter.

I-SPY points: 30

Date:

TEAL

The Teal is our smallest duck. They are never far from water and nest in thick vegetation beside bogs and pools on northern moorland. During winter they form large flocks and gather to feed on estuaries and adjacent grassland.

I-SPY points: 20

Date: _____

REED WARBLER

This summer migrant is a small brownish bird with a paler underside. The delicate looking bill is quite long. They nest only in reed beds - a major host for the Cuckoo. Listen for the chattering song.

I-SPY points: 20

Date: _____

SEDGE WARBLER

This warbler is a widely seen summer visitor from Africa. It's not shy or quiet and can often be spotted singing its random song from a bush at the edge of a reedbed. It can be distinguished from other warblers by the creamy stripe above its eye.

I-SPY points: 15

Date: _____

REED BUNTING

This bird lives in wetlands and nests in plants along the waters edge. In the breeding season, it is often to be seen singing loudly from the top of a reed or bulrush stem. It feeds on both seeds and insects but is currently suffering a serious decline in its population.

I-SPY points: 40

Date: _____

GREY HERON

The Grey Heron is easy to recognize even in flight. It flies with slow, lazy-looking wing beats and its long legs trail out behind. It is often mobbed by smaller birds.

I-SPY points: 15

Date: _____

BLACK-HEADED GULL

These common gulls are not only seen at the coast. During the winter, you can see them in most areas.

Look carefully, what colour are their heads in winter?

I-SPY points: 10

Double with answer

Date: _____

ARCTIC TERN

and the Common Tern are quite hard to tell apart so birdwatchers often group them together under the name 'Comic Tern'. Look out for their bouncing flight and forked tails.

I-SPY points: 40

Date: _____

COMMON TERN

Nicknamed the "sea-swallow", these graceful birds frequently hover over water before plunging down for a fish.

I-SPY points: 15

Date: _____

BRENT GOOSE

This goose is about the size of a large duck. They are usually seen around coastal mudflats where they feed mainly on eel grass during the winter. They are winter visitors to UK, escaping the cold of Russia and Greenland.

I-SPY points: 25

Date: _____

18

SHELDUCK

The bold colours of this bird make it easily recognizable even at a distance. It is usually found around coastal estuaries. Look out for the red knob at the base of the male's beak.

I-SPY points: 15

Date:_____

MUTE SWAN

This bird is quite unmistakable. It has been said that it is the heaviest bird capable of flying long distances.

Male and female are often given special names - what?

I-SPY points: 5

Double with answer

Date:_____

GREYLAG GOOSE

The Greylag is the largest and bulkiest of the wild geese native to the UK. With pink legs, large head, almost triangular orange-pink bill it's easy to identify.

I-SPY points: 10

Date: _____

OYSTERCATCHER

With its bright red bill, red legs, red eyes and black and white plumage, the Oystercatcher is easy to recognize at the coast. Listen for its loud piping call.

I-SPY points: 10

Date: _____

RINGED PLOVER

In the winter, these attractive little shore birds are found along muddy estuaries. For the rest of the year, look for them along sandy or shingly coasts.

I-SPY points: 15

Date: _____

DUNLIN

These little birds are common shore birds and may be seen in large flocks. You can see them dashing about the mud probing for food with their beaks.

I-SPY points: 15

Date: _____

REDSHANK

This is another common wading bird and, as its name suggests, it has red legs as well as a reddish base to its bill. They feed on estuaries during the winter.

I-SPY points: 15

Date: _____

COMMON SANDPIPER

With its white underside, brownish back, and its habit of bobbing up and down when it is on the ground, this bird is quite easy to recognize.

I-SPY points: 15

Date: _____

KINGFISHER

Although these birds have a striking, orange-coloured breast, when you see them in flight they look like small electric-blue arrows. They hunt small fish and invertebrates from riverside perches and nest at the end of tunnels that they dig in vertical banks.

I-SPY points: 20

Date: _____

DIPPER

The Dipper is a small brown bird with a white breast; it lives by fast flowing streams and shallow swift rivers. It bobs up and down on the bank prior to walking into the water where it uses its wings and sharp claws to stabilise itself while hunting insect larvae on the river bed.

I-SPY points: 40

Date: _____

BEWICK'S SWAN

These are our smallest swans but they undertake an epic journey travelling thousands of miles from from Siberia.

I-SPY points: 50

Date: _____

GREY WAGTAIL

Grey Wagtails have conspicuous yellow patches on their breasts and rumps. They are found by fast-flowing streams and often nest under bridges.

I-SPY points: 20

Date: _____

SAND MARTIN

In general shape, this bird looks like a House Martin but it is brown in colour above and has a white underside with a brown bar across its chest. It nests in burrows in sandy cliffs.

I-SPY points: 20

Date: _____

LITTLE GREBE

Another bird which delights in man-made lakes and waterways, they are often seen on quiet parts of canal systems. If alarmed they will dive and emerge a fair distance from the perceived danger.

I-SPY points: 25

Date: _____

AVOCET

This bird was almost extinct in the UK but conservation action brought it back from a few pairs in 1940 to over 800 today. It eats aquatic insects and larvae using its specialised bill.

I-SPY points: 50

Date: _____

WHITE-FRONTED GOOSE

It is unusual in that, two distinct populations visit the British Isles but only between October and March and do not breed.

I-SPY points: 30

Date: _____

TURNSTONE

A small but sturdy bird that spends its time doing what its name says, turning over stones using its strong bill to search for a meal. Notice the bright orange-red legs.

I-SPY points: 25

Date: _____

WIGEON

Are easily located by their unmistakable whistling call and flocks of thousands can be readily seen in winter as residents are supplemented by migrants from Russia and the East.

I-SPY points: 25

Date: _____

CORMORANT

These large birds nest on sea cliffs but they may be seen quite far inland on rivers. Watch out for them holding out their wings to dry after they have been diving for food.

I-SPY points: 15

Date: _____

SHAG

The Shag is smaller than the Cormorant and is rarely seen away from the coast. In the spring the bird boasts a crest on its head. The plumage appears dark green and oily.

I-SPY points: 15

Date: _____

26

HERRING GULL

The Herring Gull is a large, heavily built bird with pink legs and a yellow bill bearing a bright red spot on the underside. It is found mainly at the coast.

I-SPY points: 10

Date: _____

GREAT BLACK-BACKED GULL

The Great Black-backed Gull is even bigger and more powerful than the Herring Gull. It will even attack other birds, especially their chicks in the breeding season. It is almost always a solitary bird, but is commonly seen in mixed gull flocks.

I-SPY points: 15

Date: _____

KITTIWAKE

This medium-sized gull is noted for its black wing-tips. The Kittiwake is a strictly coastal gull and spends the winter months out at sea.

I-SPY points: 25

Date: _____

PUFFIN

The Puffin is recognised by everybody. In March they arrive at their traditional breeding colonies on the coast where they nest in tunnels. They leave in August to spend the winter far out to sea.

I-SPY points: 25

Date: _____

RAZORBILL

It is not always easy to tell Guillemots and Razorbills apart unless they are in mixed colonies, when this bird looks blacker and rather bigger than the Guillemot.

I-SPY points: 20

Date: _____

COMMON GULL

A smaller version of the herring gull, it is abundant in coastal regions and in some eastern counties. They are often seen in towns and on housing estates in winter.

I-SPY points: 5

Date: _____

FULMAR

This grey and white seabird only comes to land to breed. It is present at its breeding sites for most of the year where it glides low over the sea looking for a meal. It mostly feeds on waste fish from trawlers.

I-SPY points: 20

Date: _____

GUILLEMOT

When they sit upon rocks at the coast, this member of the auk family resemble penguins. They nest on bare ledges on sea cliffs. They are fast fliers and good swimmers.

I-SPY points: 20

Date: _____

EIDER DUCK

The Eider is a true seaduck, rarely found inland. They nest on the ground, usually on small islands for safety. Until quite recently, their old down lined nests were collected, cleaned and used as quilts.

I-SPY points: 30

Date: _____

GANNET

The Gannet is our largest seabird with a wingspan of up to 180cms! These birds dive for fish and are shaped like arrows, everything is streamlined and designed to pierce the water. They nest in huge numbers on steep cliffs but can often be seen from the shore.

I-SPY points: 25

Date: _____

PEREGRINE

This fast-flying, anchor-shaped falcon feeds mainly on birds such as pigeons and doves which it catches in flight. It swoops down on its victim and is the fastest creature in the world.

I-SPY points: 50

Date: _____

STOCK DOVE

Stock Doves are found in farmland, parks, the edges of woods, cliffs, ruined buildings and even among sand dunes. Unlike woodpigeons they nest in holes and feed mainly on seeds.

I-SPY points: 15

Date: _____

GOLDEN EAGLE

The sheer size of this bird is usually enough to give it away. It has broad wings with 'fingered' tips on which it soars while looking for live prey like mountain hares and carrion. It is estimated that around 400 pairs live in Scotland, with a few visiting Northern England each year looking for new territories to expand into.

How does the bird get its name?

I-SPY points: 35
Double with answer
Date: _____

HEN HARRIER

This is the female, drab in comparison to the male who has beautiful blue-grey plumage and a white belly with a yellow eye making him very distinctive. They tend to breed on moorlands and at other times can be found gliding slowly over coastal fields and marshes.

I-SPY points: 30
Date: _____

MERLIN

This falcon is smaller and faster than a kestrel, it hunts down small moorland birds like larks and pipits which it spots from shrubs, stunted trees, and sometimes fenceposts. During the winter it frequents our coastal grasslands where it preys on winter migrants.

I-SPY points: 40

Date: _____

CURLEW

This is our largest wader. It nests on moorlands and spends the rest of the year at the coast where it uses its long, curved bill to probe in the mud for worms and shrimps. Its name comes from its 'Cooer-Ieeoo' call.

I-SPY points: 25

Date: _____

SNIPE

This long-billed bird is best known for its habit of 'drumming' during the breeding season. It flies up and then dives with its outer tail feathers spread out to make a throbbing noise.

I-SPY points: 25

Date: _____

DOTTEREL

The Dotterel is an unusual member of the Plover family because the roles during breeding are reversed – the male bird guards the eggs and the Female has brighter plumage.

I-SPY points: 50

Date: _____

GOLDEN PLOVER

A medium-sized plover with an upstanding posture and amazing gold and black summer plumage. In winter they gather in great numbers and fly about in formation. During the summer they are breeding on moorlands but move to lowland fields to over winter.

I-SPY points: 20

Date: _____

HOODED CROW

Unlike Carrion Crows, "Hoodies" often gather in flocks. They have adapted to a harsh life and will feed on carrion but generally they are omnivorous.

I-SPY points: 15

Date: _____

SHORT-EARED OWL

Short-eared Owls are found in open country such as moorland. The word 'ear' refers to tufts of feathers on the head of the bird which are not the owl's real ears.

I-SPY points: 40

Date: _____

RAVEN

The Raven is the largest member of the crow family, larger even than a buzzard! It is completely black with a large bill and a diamond-shaped tail.

I-SPY points: 30

Date: _____

MEADOW PIPIT

This small brown bird has a longish tail which it flicks as it runs along the ground. It is usually found in open grassland or moorland.

I-SPY points: 15

Date: _____

TREE PIPIT

The Tree Pipit sings as it flies from perch to perch. It resembles a small thrush covered in brown streaks even on its back; it has pink legs and a pale stripe above the eye. It's a common summer visitor and populates our heath, moorland and young tree plantations eating small insects and berries.

I-SPY points: 20

Date:_____

STONECHAT

This black, white and orange bird is found in heaths, commons and moors. It gets its name from its call which sounds like two pebbles being knocked together.

I-SPY points: 15

Date:_____

WHEATEAR

The male Wheatear has a grey back, white rump, black face stripes and orange-pink chest, the female is paler and lacks the black cheeks. These birds are summer migrants from Africa and are commonly found in open moorland.

I-SPY points: 15

Date: _____

RED GROUSE

Also called the Willow Grouse but they are always found on heather moorland. When disturbed, they fly low with a call which sounds like 'Go Back! Go Back!'

I-SPY points: 15

Date: _____

BLACK GROUSE

The male and female, both with a distinctive lyre-shaped tail, are often called 'Black Cock' and 'Grey Hen'. They are rare even on their upland moreland habitat – and are very sensitive to disturbance.

I-SPY points: 50

Date: _____

PTARMIGAN

If you are lucky enough to see a male Ptarmigan in winter, it is likely to have changed its plumage from dark brown to all white. They are found on heather moors.

I-SPY points: 50

Date: _____

BUZZARD

Conservationists have triumphed! Buzzards can once again regularly be seen wheeling over all kinds of open country either singly or in small family groups after their number had fallen. Listen for their 'mewing' call.

I-SPY points: 25

Date: _____

SPARROWHAWK

Look for the Sparrowhawk as it dashes along and over hedgerows, it's trying to catch small birds by surprise. The female Sparrowhawk is larger and browner than males.

I-SPY points: 25

Date: _____

KESTREL

It is easy to see why this bird gets its country name of 'Windhover'. Look out for them hovering by roads and motorways searching for insects and small mammals to pounce on.

I-SPY points: 5

Date: _____

LAPWING

Flocks of Lapwings can be seen feeding on pasture and ploughed fields. They need undisturbed fields such as meadows and set-aside for nesting. Although their upper parts are greenish, in flight they look black and white.

Can you think of two other common names for this bird?

I-SPY points: 30
Double with answer

Date: _____

SPOTTED FLYCATCHER

Spotted Flycatchers arrive here in May and stay until August. While here they happily nest in farmyards, large gardens or open woodland. They feed by perching on tall shrubs or roofs watching for passing insects. Recent cold wet summers have not helped their population.

I-SPY points: 25

Date: _____

MARSH TIT

The Marsh Tit and Willow Tit look very similar with their black caps and, despite their names, both birds live in woodland although it is the Willow Tit that likes to be near water.

I-SPY points: 15

Date: _____

BARN OWL

This is a long-winged, night hunting bird. Its breast may be near white or rather more golden and sometimes the bird almost seems to glow in the dark. They do not hoot but screech and hiss.

I-SPY points: 40

Date: _____

LITTLE OWL

You may see Little Owls during the day sitting on a fence post looking for insects. As its name suggests, it is a small owl, at just 22cm.

I-SPY points: 25

Date: _____

GREEN WOODPECKER

This brightly coloured, greenish-yellow woodpecker may even be seen in gardens. It is sometimes called the 'Yaffle' because of its laughing song.

What is very noticeable about this bird's flight?

I-SPY points: 30

Double with answer

Date: _____

GREAT SPOTTED WOODPECKER

This black and white woodpecker has a red patch beneath its tail. It 'sings' by drumming its beak against a trunk or branch of a tree. The bird feeds on insects which it digs out from under the bark.

I-SPY points: 15

Date: _____

SKYLARK

As the male bird climbs into the air on rapidly beating wings, it produces its loud, warbling song. This song is a familiar sound of summer in open countryside and farmland.

I-SPY points: 20

Date: _____

SWALLOW

Familar birds of summer, Swallows feed by catching insects in flight. They will also swoop down over lakes and rivers to drink. Look out for their long tail streamers.

I-SPY points: 15

Date: _____

YELLOW WAGTAIL

Yellow Wagtails are found in damp fields and water meadows, gravel pits, wet moorland and farmland near water. They feed on insects and other small creatures.

I-SPY points: 20

Date: _____

SONG THRUSH

Song Thrushes are found in gardens, woods and hedgerows. The brown back and speckled breast make this an easy bird to Spy.

I-SPY points: 20

Date: _____

MISTLE THRUSH

This is our largest Thrush. It can be aggressive and will drive off birds like magpies from its territory if required. Easy to spot singing from the top of a tall tree.

I-SPY points: 10

Date: _____

FIELDFARE

Its large size, grey head and rump, and darker end to the tail make this thrush easy to recognize. These birds breed in open woodland but gather in large flocks in farmland from October to March.

I-SPY points: 15

Date: _____

REDWING

Redwings are the smallest member of the Thrush family. Large flocks inhabit open fields eating worms and also berries from the hedgerow. Not too hard to see as almost 750,000 birds arrive in the UK to overwinter until March.

I-SPY points: 15

Date: _____

CHIFFCHAFF

The Chiffchaff is a summer migrant that looks very like the Willow Warbler except that it has dark-coloured legs. But it gets its name from its song - a repetitive 'chiff-chaff, chiff-chaff'.

I-SPY points: 15

Date: _____

BLACKCAP

A handsome warbler with a beautiful song that lifts the spirits when it returns to us in spring from Northern Europe. A few spend the winter here and become regular visitors to the garden and bird table. They spend a large part of their lives in thick cover but the singing of the male gives them away. The female is similar but with a brown cap.

I-SPY points: 15

Date: _____

WHITETHROAT

With its brownish body, greyer head and distinctive white throat, this summer migrant is one of the easier warblers to recognize. It is found in woodlands and shrubbery.

I-SPY points: 15

Date: _____

BULLFINCH

An unmistakable British bird now on the RSPB Red list due to habitat decline and modern pesticides used by farmers. This gloriously pinkie-red male and his duller female were once common and a well known pest in fruit orchards where they devoured buds, seeds and insects.

I-SPY points: 30

Date:

SISKIN

The Siskin looks rather like a greenfinch, except that the male Siskin has a black crown and chin and rather more yellow colours on the underside. These birds eat the seeds of cones.

I-SPY points: 15

Date:

LINNET

These birds are greyish brown above and paler on the underside but, in spring and summer, the chest of the male bird is flushed with pink. They are found in open country where there are trees and bushes.

I-SPY points: 15

Date: _____

YELLOWHAMMER

It is the bright yellow head of the male bird which is easy to spot. Listen to his song in spring and summer, as he sits atop a hedge or gate post.

What does he seem to say?

I-SPY points: 10
Double with answer

Date: _____

CORN BUNTING

This bird is rather similar to the yellowhammer but it lacks the bright yellow colours. Its song sounds like the rattling of bunch of keys after a 'chinkchink' start.

I-SPY points: 10

Date: _____

MAGPIE

With its very long tail and bold black and white colours, this is an easy bird to recognize. You will often see them at the roadside feeding on animals that were killed on the roads.

I-SPY points: 5

Date: _____

ROOK

This is a large, glossy black bird with a long bill that has a grey base. It is often found in large flocks feeding on open farmland, or in parks and gardens.

I-SPY points: 5

Date: _____

CARRION CROW

This clever member of the Crow family is completely black, even its stout bill that can used to carry large objects. It is usually solitary but may be found in small family parties.

I-SPY points: 15

Date: _____

WOOD PIGEON

When Wood Pigeons take off, they usually make a loud clapping noise with their wings as they strike together. This is thought to help them make a fast take-off.

I-SPY points: 5

Date: _____

COLLARED DOVE

With their pinkish, fawnish, grey colour and black, collar-like mark on either side of the neck, these birds are easy to recognize. They can often be seen in gardens.

I-SPY points: 5

Date: _____

RED-LEGGED PARTRIDGE

Nicknamed by the shooting fraternity "Frenchmen", this type of partridge has been introduced into Britain from mainland Europe. It is slightly larger than our native breed and appears to thrive in farmland bounded by woods

I-SPY points: 15

Date: _____

PHEASANT

The brightly coloured male
Pheasant is unmistakable. These
birds are found in most types of
country where there are seeds and
berries to feed on.

I-SPY points: 10

Date: _____

GREY PARTRIDGE

An orange faced, plump breasted
gamebird that has joined the RSPB
Red list due to habitat loss and
modern farming methods. They
are sociable birds outside of the
breeding season and form into
groups called "Coveys" for safety.

I-SPY points: 30

Date: _____

QUAIL

At 18cms, This diminutive
gamebird comes to visit us in
the late spring and stays until
autumn. It hunts for insects in
standing crops.

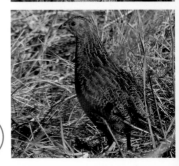

I-SPY points: 50

Date: _____

GOSHAWK

It's almost as large as a buzzard but this handsome hawk is more agile. It often hunts birds up to pigeon size by chasing them through the trees at high speed but they will also soar in order to spot mammals and birds on the ground. As usual with birds of prey, the female is larger than the male.

I-SPY points: 50

Date:

TREECREEPER

A secretive, small brown speckled bird which feeds on bugs which try to hide in the bark of trees, but not much can hide from that thin, curved beak. It feeds to the top of the tree then flies to the bottom of the next one to start climbing and feeding all over again.

I-SPY points: 30

Date:

LESSER SPOTTED WOODPECKER

This is like a smaller version of the Great Spotted: the male bird has a red cap. The drumming song is quieter and more rapid than that of its larger cousin.

I-SPY points: 25

Date: _____

NUTHATCH

The nuthatch will readily visit garden feeders. In the wild woodland it scrambles around on tree trunks and branches looking for insects.

I-SPY points: 20

Date: _____

CUCKOO

The Cuckoo is more often heard than seen: they are sometimes mistaken for birds of prey in flight. They are best known for their habit of laying their eggs in the nests of other birds.

I-SPY points: 25

Date: _____

56

Woodland, Forests and Copses

GOLDCREST

This is a tiny, greenish-coloured bird that is usually seen flitting from branch to branch on larches and other coniferous trees. If you see one, look for the yellow strip with black lines on either side on the bird's head.

I-SPY points: 30

Date:

JAY

This brightly coloured member of the crow family is usually a shy bird and you are lucky if you see one flying between patches of woodland. Sometimes, though, they do turn up in gardens.

I-SPY points: 15

Date:

JACKDAW

Smaller than a rook or a crow and with a greyish head and rather untidy appearance, the Jackdaw is quite easy to identify. Its harsh 'keeaw' call is also very noticeable.

I-SPY points: 5

Date:

TAWNY OWL

This is the woodland owl which makes the familiar hooting noise. If you see mobs of small birds seemingly attacking an ivy-covered tree, there may well be a Tawny Owl roosting there.

I-SPY points: 40
Date: _____

TURTLE DOVE

The Turtle Dove is a summer visitor from Africa which is usually found in open woodland in the south-east and Kent. They are more often heard than seen, and make a pleasant purring sound.

I-SPY points: 25
Date: _____

LITTLE EGRET

Only 10 years ago it was rare to see a Little Egret. It is now commonly sighted in marshes and rivers, but most often in large numbers at favoured coastal sites.

I-SPY points: 25

Date: _____

BITTERN

The brown and black Bitterns usually frequent reedbeds and similar marshy areas, and feed on amphibians, reptiles, insects and fish. The male has a distinctive low-pitched mating call, a far-carrying "boom".

I-SPY points: 30

Date: _____

RED KITE

This reddy coloured bird of prey is quite easily recognized from its 'floating' flight, 165cm wingspan and forked tail. Since the 1980s it has been brought back from national extinction and in some areas can be seen in small flocks.

I-SPY points: 25

Date: _____

OSPREY

Ospreys are rare summer visitors to Speyside in Scotland, Bassenthwaite in Cumbria, Rutland Water in Leicestershire and the Glaslyn valley in Wales, these are the sanctuaries where, with luck, the birds will nest and a good view can be had. They feed by swooping down and grasping a fish from the water.

I-SPY points: 50

Date: _____

HOOPOE

With its curved bill, black and white wings, bright pinkish plumage and large crest, this foreign visitor is very distinctive. It occasionally arrives along the South coast in error! So far it has not nested here but with Britain's climate change, who knows?

I-SPY points: 50

Date: _____

RING-NECKED PARAKEET

These handsome parrots were introduced to south-east England in the early 1970s and have now increased to many thousands thanks to abundant bird table offerings, and garden fruit.

I-SPY points: 20

Date: _____

GREAT BUSTARD

Persecuted to local extinction in the 1840s, the Bustard is on the way back thanks to a well guarded conservation project (birds are individually tagged) which, since 2004 has released over 50 adult birds onto Salisbury Plain. In 2009 the first chicks were raised, as seen in the picture.

I-SPY points: 50

Date:

WAXWING

The waxwing visits when winter food supplies dwindle in its regular home territory of Scandinavia. It comes here for berries and fruit such as Hawthorn and Rowan.

I-SPY points: 50

Date:

Index

First published by Michelin Maps and Guides 2009
© Michelin, Proprietaires-Editeurs 2009.
Michelin and the Michelin Man are registered
Trademarks of Michelin.
Created and produced by Blue Sky Publishing Limited.
All rights reserved. No part of this publication may be
reproduced, copied or transmitted in any form without
the prior consent of the publisher.
Print services by FingerPrint International Book
production - fingerprint@pandora.be
The publisher gratefully acknowledges the contribution
of the I-Spy team: Camilla Lovell, Graeme Newton-Cox,
Ruth Neilson and Jordan Watts in the production of
this title.
The publisher gratefully acknowledges the contribution of
Anthony Dixon, Brian Rafferty, David Whistlecraft, Colin
Selway, Dave Kjaer, David Whistlecraft, Gary Thoburn,
Jim Woods, John Anderson, Mark Bicknell, Neil Boulton,
Sean Johnston, Shirley Roulston, Terry Gunby, Tom
Marshall, Trevor Gunby and Unitaw Limited who provided
the photographs used in this book. Other images in the public
domain and used under a creative commons licence.
Reprinted 2011   10 9 8 7

I-SPY
One Token
715126

HOW TO GET YOUR I-SPY CERTIFICATE AND BADGE

Every time you score 1000 points or more in an I-Spy book, you can apply for a certificate

Here's what to do, step by step:

Certificate

- Ask an adult to check your score

- Ask his or her permission to apply for a certificate

- Apply online to www.ispymichelin.com

- Enter your name and address and the completed title

- We will send you back via e mail your certificate for the title

Badge

- Each I-Spy title has a cut out (page corner) token at the back of the book

- Collect five tokens from different I-Spy titles

- Put Second Class Stamps on two strong envelopes

- Write your own address on one envelope and put a £1 coin inside it (for protection). Fold, but do not seal the envelope, and place it inside the second envelope

- Write the following address on the second envelope, seal it carefully and post to:

I-Spy Books
Michelin Maps and Guides
Hannay House
39 Clarendon Road
Watford
WD17 1JA